THE BARSTOOL GUIDE TO JERKS

Losers and Abusers to Avoid

By David Dasnod

Disclaimer

The Barstool Guide to Jerks was written by a bartender for people who suffer from being exposed to jerks. The author of The Barstool Guide to Jerks is not a licensed mental health professional or affiliated with any licensed medical organization.

The content in The Barstool Guide to Jerks is intended for entertainment purposes only and should be treated accordingly. The content is based on the author's own experiences and is shared in good faith. However, the information contained within should not be used to replace or modify the diagnosis or treatment recommendations of any licensed mental health professional or medical practitioner. Please consult with your doctor, therapist or mental health professional before applying any ideas or suggestions from The Barstool Guide to Jerks to your own situation.

The author of The Barstool Guide to Jerks shall not be liable for any damage resulting from the use or misuse of information or suggestions contained within. By reading The Barstool Guide to Jerks you agree to these conditions and are reading the said book at your own risk.

With that said: If you suspect you may have a family member or loved one who's a jerk, I encourage you to learn all you can about jerks, learn to master the art of assertive communication and surround yourself with a good supply of hard liquor.

CONTENTS

Jerks are the monkeys of man in comparison to others that have grown out of their jerkhood.

David Dasnod 2019

My Definition of a Jerk to Avoid

1: A jerk is often a male who lacks respect or regard for others and uses them to gain something for himself without giving anything of value back in exchange. A jerk holds little value for others outside of that person's usefulness. The jerk is self-centered and is only concerned with his own needs.

2: A reactive, unstable, reckless, obnoxious and or exploitative person. The jerk is characterized by inappropriate behaviors that may lead to distress in anyone exposed to his behaviors. He can be rude or obnoxious towards others without any concern for those around him. He usually treats others unkindly.

3: Because jerks are jerks they often find themselves isolated, alone and in need of attention. And because jerks are jerks they are also in need of major behavior modifications. But mostly, jerks just need to be left alone, isolated and avoided whenever possible.

PREFACE

This book is the product of years standing behind a bar listening to hours upon hours of people complaining, crying, joking and laughing about one another and the jerks they knew. It's a condensed collection of all those conversations that took place in the wee hours when all the really great conversations take place. I came to believe that angels speak through drunken hearts if you remain sober enough to listen.

I found a little bit of myself each night behind that bar when people came in to vent and exchange stories with one another. As we poked fun at the jerks that came through that bar and into our lives, I found myself seeking and discovering parts of myself. I learned a lot about myself and my own jerkish tendencies during those years. I began to see how much we are all connected and in many ways very much alike.

I hope this book helps to validate or refine what you already know and understand about the jerk in your life. Insight is power and maybe I can shed a little light on the subject for you and allow you to see your way out of a bad situation without stumbling over too many obstacles or people in the process. However, I don't believe this book will shed a lot of light on the meaning of life but perhaps it will help you to improve the quality of your stay here on earth just a little bit more before that final last call.

For the sake of simplicity, I have taken the liberty to assign gender pronouns to the jerk and the accommodator. I refer to the jerk as male and the accommodator as female. I hope this does not upset you. Jerks do tend to be male in most cases and accommodators tend to be female. However the roles can be any gender; male/female, female/female, male/male and even female/male orientation. I hope you do not find my choice to use these pronouns as such to be disrespectful or discourteous.

I am simply attempting to keep the reading from being confusing. It's hard at times to talk about the jerk without talking about the accommodator as well. Because without the accommodator it would be hard for the jerk to be what he is. The jerk seeks accommodators so he can continue to be a jerk. Without the accommodator, the jerk would have to learn to be responsible, respectful and a little accommodating himself in order to survive in the world we live in today. But then if the jerk wants to be ill-mannered, coarse and contemptible in behavior and appearance like a Neanderthal then I suppose he can also find a cave to live in or a bridge to live under if he likes.

The Accommodator

In order to understand the jerk, I feel it is important to understand the accommodator as well. An accommodator is someone that accommodates a jerk. The accommodator is valued by the jerk by what she can do for him. A universal characteristic of a jerk is that he fears the loss of an accommodator, once he finds one and places a lot of emphasis on maintaining or replacing that codependent arrangement. Most of what a jerk does is towards developing or maintaining an accommodator's servitude. Sometimes a jerk is rude and disrespectful because he is seeking a person that will accommodate that behavior. Anyone willing to accommodate him may find themselves in a role as a free maid or a free personal chauffeur. The jerk may even consider that person to be his own personal, living sex doll.

A jerk will seek out an accommodator because she tends to be overly accommodating to him. She is easy to get along with because she possesses a passive disposition. The jerk seeks her because she tends to sacrifice the quality of her life for the betterment of his. She consistently provides a jerk with assistance or privileges without receiving anything of any value in return. She tries to get along with the jerk by suppressing her own feelings and needs in order to avoid conflict and in hopes that the jerk may become dependent on her.

By thinking that if the jerk depends on her she will remain significant to him and thus he won't leave her. She allows and welcomes his demands, his abuse, his jerkishness. She wants to believe that he acts the way he does because he relies on her and she has disappointed him. She gives and gives just to remain in the good graces of the jerk. She believes that if she can get the jerk dependent on her then she can feel significant to him. And once she believes that he is reliant on her she does everything in her power to maintain that dependency for as long as she can until she breaks or until she destroys herself in the process.

The jerk will often make his accommodator feel anxious, causing her to worry often. The jerk is a master at making his accommodator neurotic with his behaviors. By promoting emotional instability the jerk forces an accommodator to walk on eggshells. By accommodating the jerk the accommodator may also reduce some anxiety for herself. She believes that it is better to go ahead and accommodate the jerk than it is to put up with the verbal or physical abuse that would follow if she didn't. She becomes brainwashed through abusive conditioning. She feels emotional discomfort when she goes against what the jerk expects of her. As long as she can make him happy she feels safe.

The accommodator may be punished if she does not cater sufficiently to the jerk's needs. She tries to predict those needs and feels compelled to meet them. Her punishment may consist of a variety of forms, including physical abuse, outbursts of rage, guilt, blame, criticism, and emotional withdrawal. But the real purpose of this punishment is to enforce compliance with his wishes.

So the accommodator works hard to please the jerk. She finds it hard to have her own views and values. She yields to his opinions, worries about how he feels about her, and is often depressed or anxious. She does not believe she has inherent value but that her self-worth is based on what the jerk may think of her. Her self-image is based on the jerk's treatment of her and therefore she holds inaccurate ideas about herself and who she is. Being exposed to a jerk's behaviors over time can eventually make an accommodator mentally and physically ill.

She may fear that she is inherently insensitive, selfish, defective, fearful, unloving, overly demanding, hard to satisfy, inhibited, or worthless based on what the jerk says to her and how he treats her. If she tries to empower herself and stand up to him, she will be afraid that the jerk will consider her selfish because she will be acting too assertive. So eventually she caves in under the stress of accommodating an exploitive jerk and becomes his personal slave.

INTRODUCTION

Recognizing a jerk is not that complicated because people usually know a jerk when they see one. Generally, a jerk is loud, rude and disrespectful. He is likely to be threatening, demeaning, insulting, humiliating, exploiting and physically or verbally abusive. A jerk can be unpleasant, inhospitable, and downright difficult to be around.

He will place the blame on others and refuse to accept any responsibility for his actions. He is quick to anger if embarrassed due to his over-inflated ego. The Jerk usually has a sadistic sense of humor and as a rule, he is a sexist. A jerk lacks positive social skills because he is insensitive, selfish, inconsiderate and self-centered. He can be offensive, self-serving and mean. Most of the time, a jerk is completely clueless about how unpleasant a person he really is.

The Jerk is born a jerk. He is brought into this world needy, selfish and self-centered. He plays with the new world around him and quickly learns to manipulate it in order to get what he needs or wants. He soon learns what works and what doesn't work. He tries to learn better ways of manipulation through experimentation and may even adopt a few techniques along the way from other jerks as he grows older. As a child, he tries everything he can think of to manipulate the world around him because, as a child, he is unable to acquire everything he wants on his own.

He learns that others can usually provide the things he needs and desires. He discovers new forms of manipulation that seem to work for him and uses them over and over again. These manipulative behaviors are soon reinforced by practicing them with success every day. By practicing his style of interacting with others, it soon becomes a habit and he manages to get through life by using the behavior style he has developed. Sometimes his manipulative style works and sometimes it doesn't. He simply accepts it and moves on.

Those of us that learn to communicate assertively with others without manipulating them grow into well-adjusted adults. Sometimes the jerk is fortunate enough to have some guidance while growing up. And sometimes the jerk never learns how to interact with others without manipulating them. So he continues to struggle to get what he needs or wants but chooses to remain an immature jerk anyway.

He is likely to blame anything and everything as a contributing factor to his jerk-like behavior but it is really just a contributing excuse. The jerk is a jerk because he chooses to be. It's easy to be a jerk. It's easy to remain a jerk because a jerk doesn't have to struggle to become a mature adult. An immature jerk prefers to be around other immature people because that is the level of development he can relate to. Most of the time the jerk will eventually grow out of his jerkhood and tire of being around immature people. But sometimes a jerk may go through his entire life seeking to be around immature people because he remains immature too. That is why young jerks are seldom alone but an old jerk is a lonely jerk.

It only makes sense that the jerk will be a jerk if it is advantageous to remain a jerk. As long as there is someone that enables him to be a jerk and as long as he is rewarded for being a jerk he will continue to act like a jerk. Why should he change if being a jerk is working for him? But the jerk does change with age. He is still a jerk but he develops new strategies. For example, physical aggression may be employed more often by a young jerk than by an older one. An older jerk may shift his strategy from physical aggression to verbal manipulation because it is less likely to lead to a physical confrontation. An older jerk has less energy thus is less likely to come out on top if physical aggression is provoked. Some behaviors such as attention-seeking, however, may become more apparent as the jerk ages, because he may start to noticed that no-one is paying any attention to him and intimidating others just doesn't work as well for him as it use to.

Although jerks utilize bars and pubs frequently they seldom listen to the bartender long enough to make any positive changes in their behaviors. When it comes to self-help methods for modifying one's behavior forget it. The jerk is not interested in self-help. To the jerk, it's not him that needs to change but the world needs to conform to his expectations. Self-help support groups for jerks simply don't exist. Such approaches may not be very effective anyway since jerks are likely to avoid such sessions. And besides, a group would not be very helpful because most jerks would use a group as an opportunity to practice and hone their jerkish behaviors or adopt new ones. They would likely come to groups just to brag about their exploits or seek other ways to use the group inappropriately.

There is no known magic pill to treat jerks. However, heavy pharmacotherapy could be the treatment of choice to reduce the behaviors associated with jerks but they would need to be strictly monitored for the likelihood of potential abuse. So, drugs may not be an effective treatment and would more likely contribute to their already destructive behavior. Some therapists have used hypnosis to help jerks cope with occupational issues but in most cases, a good old fashion thrashing would be the quickest and most efficient method of treatment. A good flogging would give the jerk an opportunity to rethink his behavior style and perhaps learn more constructive ways of interacting with others. However, this method of treatment is not allowed in some countries and does violate various human rights issues.

Although treatment might not be possible, an early diagnosis can assist potential jerks and family members to recognize the pattern of behaviors that reinforce adult jerk behaviors. Educating people about the character traits of jerks may prevent some early mild cases from developing into full-grown jerks. Further research in prevention needs to focus on variables such as proper communication skills, learning when to speak and when not to, when to use the words please and thank you, social etiquette, personal boundaries, general respect and the laws of consequences.

Jerks in the Wild

It's sad but new breeds of Jerks are being identified daily. Jerkologists don't even know how many types of jerks there are in our society today. As of today, there has not even been an estimate made but I would guess that there is approximately one jerk for every three barstools in the world. I don't know how many barstools there are so there isn't really any way for me to even guess how many jerks that would be. But I'm pretty sure that 95 percent of them are male and that 20 percent of those jerks still live with mommy and daddy. However, only a small sample of the world's bars have been explored as of yet but jerks are known to thrive in just about any environment on earth.

New jerks are born each day but not all of them remain jerks their entire lives. Many grow out of their jerkhood while it may seem that the rest of them continue to grow into their jerk like characteristics and develop permanent jerk type personalities. Instead of growing out of bad patterns of behavior, jerks can actually grow into them.

Jerks need accommodators in order to remain jerks, otherwise they have to adapt, meaning that they have to grow out of their jerk like behaviors and develop a respectful regard for others. Jerks thrive where they can continue to be jerks and they tend to congregate where they are likely to find suitable accommodators, and that is in bars, nightclubs, and taverns.

Jerkologist could spend centuries trying to catalog all the different jerk types on Earth. Different cultures create different types of jerks and some jerk like behaviors are not considered to be jerk like at all in some cultures. So It would be hard to establish a universal standard for jerk identification. However, there are typical jerk like behaviors that are accepted universally throughout the world. We all know jerks when we encounter them so regardless of the culture from which the jerk is found it would seem easy to identify the different types of jerks. Seeing is believing and this is where we should start if we should ever attempt to identify and catalog all the different jerk types on planet earth.

Every jerk is unique, however, there are some common behavior patterns. The following list contains prominent attributes of some of the more common jerks observed in bars and taverns throughout the United States. These categories of traits may seem like traits of an unpleasant, immature, uncultured person and this is no accident. Most jerks are unpleasant, immature and uncultured people. Approximately 4 in 10 people you would meet in a bar are jerks (aside from country bars where the ratio is much higher). A jerk may not exhibit all of the traits mentioned in these descriptions and on the other hand the presence of one or more of these traits does not necessarily make someone a jerk; meaning, most of the people you would meet in a bar don't quite fit these stereotypical models for jerks but their behaviors can be similar at times.

These general depictions are not intended for any kind of diagnosis purpose; after all, we really are not trying to help jerks get better here, but are simply for the identification of jerk types by non-jerks. They are offered in the hope that you might find it easier to recognize a true jerk when you meet one; thus saving you some time, money and perhaps your sanity.

The following assortment is a collection of various jerk types you may easily find lurking in the world around you. This information is to act as a guide to help you better understand some of the various types of jerks and to provide you with a common base for communicating with others about jerks on your own.

THE LOSER JERK
TYPE

The loser jerk seldom pays for anything and expects you to use your resources all the time. This jerk doesn't want a relationship; he just wants to use you up and move on and if you want to call that a relationship, that's okay with him. He will tell you whatever he thinks you want to hear in order to get what he wants. He only gives when there is something in it for him and will likely change back into his old jerk personality once he gets what he wants. He is disrespectful to you whenever he uses praise, gratitude, and compliments to get what he wants from you.

He tries to get you to feel sorry for him by whining and complaining. He intimidates by yelling and arguing with you. He interrogates you with his endless questions and accusations and sucks up your attention by talking too much. He is the jerk that feels that if he spends any money on you that it is only fair that you sleep with him. He is also the jerk that expects to hook up with you after being out late with other people.

The loser jerk usually fails to sustain a consistent work history or honor financial obligations because he is not mature enough to be responsible for himself. He is uninterested in dealing with "mundane" matters such as cleaning, paying bills, etc. as long as he has someone else to do it for him. And if you do anything for him, he has a tendency to take your services for granted. He may believe that housework and cooking is woman's work, and as sad as it may be this jerk is not even close to extinction. He lives entirely in the present. He thrives on entertainment and excitement and will stir things up to create it.

ALL AMERICAN

The All American is usually an ultra-conservative jerk who came from a middle to upper-class family. He was likely a high school jock that drank cans of nasty domestic beer every weekend and dated snooty cheerleaders. Years of social brainwashing has left him emotionally detached from himself as well as others. He is shallow minded lacking any depth of personality and is only concerned with what is safely obvious.

He relies on his possessions and extensive travels to measure his self-worth. This over privileged drunken letterman was extremely sheltered from discomfort and tends to be inherently prejudiced towards anyone in a lower income bracket. This jerk is all about appearances. He is in love with his social-image and exhibits an exaggerated sense of self-importance. This jerk has a tendency to be quite arrogant. He seeks the admiration of others and expects special treatment because he believes he is exceptional.

This jerk maintains a lot of relationships and is likely to sustain many acquaintances. He is afraid to damage any relationship fearing that he may need their alliance someday. This fear of offending someone causes him to lack spontaneity, originality or any hints of individuality.

He has a set of conventional principles and expectations pertaining to his particular social group. It is difficult for him to tolerate any criticism or negative feedback about himself or his things and is displeased with anything that does not meet his high standards. This jerk is constantly suggesting or implying things you should change to improve the way you look. If he isn't hounding you about your appearance he's concerned about the company you keep. When it comes to his image he can become quite the control freak. If you are not careful he will manipulate you into becoming his little social puppet; hosting parties, arranging events and working hard to promote him in all his glory.

AVOIDER JERK

If emotions where water, this jerk would be the horse that, if lead to it, wouldn't drink it. He would also be careful not to get his hooves wet either. He views close or warm friendships as though he is window shopping for a better life. Expressing deep emotions isn't easy for this jerk. The Avoider Jerk tends to be very independent and he comes off as being 'secretive' when asked about himself. This jerk is afraid of committing himself in any relationship making it difficult to feel close to him; even though it's what he thirst for the most.

You may recognize the Avoider Jerk because he prefers solitude and privacy so he will likely prefer an isolated table somewhere off in the shadows where it's easy to remain tight-lipped and reserved. Passive in appearance he may be harboring some resentment toward himself for sabotaging his own relationships or towards others for making relationships seem so easy. The Avoider Jerk simply does not like confrontation. Resolving conflicts is too much work, it involves communicating what you want. Letting others know what you want involves trust and the whole mess is too uncomfortable for him. So he averts having to deal with it by avoiding it altogether by staying to himself.

Developing a relationship with this feral breed will take a lot of patients. His emotional footing isn't very stable and may buck away at the slightest pressure to be more affectionate. Unless you are looking for something shallow and casual, a relationship with the Avoider Jerk may be a waste of time because this horse just won't drink.

BAD BOY

The Bad Boy is an uninhibited rebel with an appealing sense of naughtiness about him. He tends to be unconventional and sly mannered with a sexual innuendo and a wink trailing after everything he says. But this jerk isn't really a jerk in the typical sense. He's not really bad as alleged but more often simply misunderstood. There is a slight difference between a true jerk and a Bad Boy. A true jerk intentionally treats women badly whereas a 'Bad Boy' doesn't necessarily mean that he is 'bad to you'.   This sexy rule-breaker is appealing to good girls because it is believed by some that the intensity that impels the Bad Boy to fly off into a burst of anger, and other deep emotions, is the intensity that makes him such a fervent lover. At least that's what women who like bad boys are hoping.

But the Bad Boy is a jerk in that he's a typical loser type. His rebellious attitude and lack of discipline will not make him very popular in social settings. His lack of social skills will leave him awkwardly struggling in the real world where cooperation and negotiation rule. Eventually, the Bad Boy is bound to self-destruct, and you don't want to be anywhere near him when it happens.

BAR HOPPER

Superficial relationships are all this jerk has ever known. This jerk does not understand that relationships are created and take time. A healthy and fulfilling relationship is not like a bar where he can just walk in and out of, it takes time to create a lasting relationship. This jerk is confused and needs to learn that a relationship with a person is not like a relationship with a barstool where you can plop down on the one nearest to you and just get up and leave it when you're done.

It doesn't take a lot to make this jerk feel connected to you because he is very shallow when it comes to intimate feelings. By hopping from one relationship to another, he hopes he will eventually find someone that can bring him happiness and ease his loneliness. Unable to ease his inner discomfort he quickly moves from one person to the next, looking for a nice cozy person to hang out with. This jerk is desperately seeking a connection with someone but is unwilling to take the time to create one. This rapid attachment and detachment is a sign of emotional immaturity and he will likely toss a tip in your jar and depart from you just as fast as he came without notice.

BARRACUDA

The Barracuda plays women in a game of catch-and-release. He gets an ego boost by snagging his quarry into his net of charisma and tries to see how many women he can catch at a time. He throws out his verbal lures like chum in hopes to get a bite or two and once his prey is secured in his net he is casting his line for another catch.

He loves to get his photo taken with his catches to show to his friends. And he likes to post his trophy catches on his walls, in his wallet or just about any-place where they will be seen and admired by other like sportsmen.

Older Barracudas are more or less solitary, while the young and half-grown jerks of this type frequently congregate. They prey primarily on women with emotional problems such as depression, low self-esteem issues and the like. The Barracuda is an oppor-tunistic jerk, relying on an accommodating crowd to bag his trophies. He's not likely to be found in low profile bars where the catch is limited but prefers the larger more popular clubs.

BIGMOUTH

This jerk is a loudmouthed, gossipy troublemaker. He likes to spread gossip and will not keep anything secret. He is nosy and pries into your personal affairs just so he can deliberately stir things up. The Bigmouth is meddlesome, intrusive and nothing but trouble.

When you meet him, he appears to be pleasant and respectful. But it's not long before he uses your words against you in many creative and malicious ways. You have to be careful what you say and do around a Bigmouth. What you say in confidence is soon broadcast over the bar and beyond. Most people couldn't care less about your personal affairs or your opinions. But those that would care to know will know what you said and perhaps with a twist to it.

The Bigmouth feels he has a right to sacrifice anyone and everyone to make himself feel significant. So don't talk about your life or complain about anything or anyone if you are within earshot of him. If you try to stay out of his little game he will try to suck you into one with his two-faced manipulative ways. I don't know why people tolerate these jerks. But they do. I suppose people find him entertaining.

If you just come out and tell the Bigmouth that he is a Bigmouth he will act hurt and really start sucking up the attention at your expense even though everyone knows he is a loudmouth jerk. But if you ignore him he will use it as an excuse to pry to gain more ammunition to use against you. The best way to neutralize a bigmouth is to pass out earplugs to everyone and stop listening to his imprudent, incessantly harmful gabble. Stop feeding his significance and he will quickly move on to better hunting grounds.

BIGOT JERK

This nasty narrow-minded jerk can be identified by his strong loyalty to his breed. He is strongly partial to members of his own group, gender, race or political party. He easily bonds with anyone that shares his values and beliefs and is intolerant to anyone that holds different opinions than his own. The characteristics of his tribal signals consist of racial slurs and jokes of poor taste.

Arguing with the Bigot Jerk will only encourage him to defend his territory. The Bigot is afraid of change. He is afraid that anything other than what he is familiar with, will become the norm. He believes that any change in the status quo will threaten his way of life and it makes him uncomfortable. The thought of this change fills him with insecurity about his place in a new and unfamiliar world. So he lashes out at everything that is foreign to him and remains partial to his own culture, religion, race and political party.

Unless you find yourself agreeing with the philosophy of the Bigot Jerk, the best thing to do is back away slowly. I personally can't stand closed minded bigots, but I've found you aren't going to make them see the light anytime soon.

CREEP

Although the Creep isn't too common he does come out of his little room at his mother's house now and then. If you do come across one of these guys, you will not forget him soon. Most of the time this parasitical jerk is harmless and will wander off on his own if he isn't provided with an appropriate host.

An encounter with this creature of the outer reaches of our social culture is enough to set your whole evening on edge. This jerk will appear slightly odd or even a bit weird from the start and definitely out of the ordinary. His lurking behavior creates an unpleasant feeling of apprehension or unease simply because he is hard to read and his behavior remains unpredictable. This annoying freak reeks with an unpleasant air of unentitled intimacy. He acts as though he just walked into an established relationship with you even though you have yet to be introduced. Aside from just being attracted to you, this Creep may also be hoping that you play along with him so as to give everyone in the bar the impression that he does have at least one friend in the world. BUT DO NOT ACCOMMODATE THIS JERK.

This jerk is seeking an intimate connection with

someone but isn't willing or capable of building any meaningful relationships. This Creep will suck up all the attention he can get from you, believing that your attention is affection. Although it's sad and somewhat pathetic, you have to be careful not to lead him on because what was somewhat creepy could soon become somewhat frightening. This jerk is emotionally unstable and could easily grow strongly attached to you very quickly. He can become unpredictable once he connects to you emotionally, and it doesn't take much. So unless you are comfortable having a stalker following you around go ahead and pet your new friend. It may be the start of something really Creepy.

DEPENDENT

While this jerk may be one of the easiest to get along with, he may also be one of the most difficult jerks to maintain a relationship with. This jerk lives in a fantasy world and seems naive. He requires constant reassurance and support. The Dependent lacks the confidence to go it alone. He finds it difficult to care for himself due to his discomfort in making everyday decisions. He avoids jobs that require autonomous duties and positions of responsibility.

The Dependent has an intense fear of abandonment and is usually devastated when a relationship ends. He can be very agreeable with you, bordering on submissiveness, for fear of losing your approval and support. This makes him over-sensitive to criticism. He is willing to tolerate a high degree of abuse in exchange for a sense of security.

After a few dates, he will want to move in with you. Chances are he can't afford or manage his own place. This jerk is unable to sustain himself without assistance and hopes you will feel obligated to take care of him.

This jerk is will cling to you like a tick so unless you are looking for a parasitical dependent to add to your tax return, keep your doors locked, your car keys in your pocket, change your phone number and email account and act like your not home when he comes knocking.

DAMAGED SCHLOCK

This jerk may be acting as though he has just gone through a heart-wrenching breakup in order to trigger a sympathetic reaction from you. He pretends to suffer but it's a means to mask his insensitive and noncommittal character. It's not uncommon for most jerks to pretend to be hurt after a breakup to get sympathy. Perhaps that should be expected, however, this jerk may be acting and then he may not be. He may be mending a broken heart from ten years ago or you may start to realize that this jerk's heart isn't bleeding as profusely as he lets on. He may have set in his mind to never fall in love again. He may have become bitter about relationships in general. He may even be harboring some resentment from past relationships. It's sad, but some jerks just can't give up a past relationship even though they clearly know it's over; after all, good accommodators are hard to find.

Anyone that starts dumping off his baggage before he even gets in the front door with you should be setting off your loser-jerk alarm system. If he uses the old he's not good enough for you bit, don't waste your time trying to convince this jerk that he really, really, really does deserve you. If his self-esteem is that low, throw a few beers in him and see if his self-esteem improves; if not, he is in need of a lot of fixing. Most people will eventually mend themselves after a relationship ends so this jerk may just be looking for someone to use and abuse.

Whatever his story, he may be coddling the relationships he screwed up in the past, or after a few beers, you may figure out that the Damaged Schlock just enjoys being a broken toy.

DOER

This is the guy carrying a round of drinks to the table where his friends are sitting. He's up and down all night doing stuff. If he isn't fetching drinks he's dancing. This guy has got to be doing something all the time. The Doer is outgoing, enthusiastic and excitable. He can be very blunt and straightforward and why not he's not afraid of anything and lives on the edge between risk-taking and life for the experience. He will drop what he's doing and plunge right into things that appeal to him. He might just finish a river ride with one group of friends and meet up with another group to explore some caves in the area. You may find him in an office setting, jumping from one project to the next, traveling to meetings and picking up where he left off when he gets back. He's organized and always a few steps ahead of everyone else.

The Doer is usually a very likable person with a soft persona and values the 'live and let be' philosophy of life. Rules are guidelines and he tends to promote his own belief in what's right and wrong but will not normally do anything he knows is unlawful.

However, if your Doer is a gambler or a spendthrift, look out. If he tends to chase after women then good luck keeping this guy on a leash. If he is into fast cars or motorcycles then make sure he is buying his own insurance. If whatever he is doing is appealing to him then there is no stopping him. This guy can easily become an extremist at anything and he can take you to new heights just as easily as new depths. So if you can keep up with this guy I hope you don't find yourself thrown off during the ride.

EMBARRASSING JERK

This jerk is very inconsiderate to your feelings. He will blurt out in public things you may have discussed with him in private. Or he may think it's funny to lick your face in front of your peers. The Embarrassing Jerk does things out of the blue that causes you to feel uncomfortably self-conscious.

He will do embarrassing things to you in order to draw attention to your flaws rather than his own. By diminishing your character and making you less desirable he is actually increasing his control over you. In an effort to keep you under control while in public, this jerk may eventually lash out at you, call you names, or say cruel or embarrassing things about you in private or in front of people. You will quickly learn while in public that any opinion you express may cause him to verbally attack you, either then or later when you both alone. If you stay with this loser too long, you'll soon find yourself politely smiling, saying nothing, and holding on to his arm when you're in the public eye. You'll also find yourself walking with your head down, fearful of seeing a friend who might speak to you and create another dreadful reaction from this loser.

This jerk could use a good swift kick to the marble

sack but don't make a public scene out of it.

EXECUTIVE

If you are seeking a spontaneous and fun loving evening, you would do well to avoid this conceited and self-centered jerk. He's the jerk in the suit with shiny shoes at the bar. He use to be fun to be around before he became a stuffy and boring jerk. The Executive is probably an ex-college professor that has lost his engaging disposition and is just plain, shallow and uninteresting. Sports gives him something to talk about with other men because he lacks anything original or interesting to say. He feels safe repeating things that are common knowledge.

This jerk believes it's his birthright to be the leader and loves to take charge in any situation. He is quick to verbalize his opinions and makes hasty decisions. This jerk can be forceful, intimidating, overbearing, dictatorial and abrasive. He intrusively gives orders without any concern for other people's feelings. He prefers to associate with people that are well-educated, structured and agreeable.

The Executive won't do anything for himself. Giving others things to do gives him a sense of purpose. His life would be meaningless if he didn't have an accommodator to wipe his butt. He's simply a prick in a suit. So unless you are a member of his suck-up slacker club it may be best to take your friends over to the water fountain to have your drinks.

FLAKE

The Flake is annoying and disruptive to your life. He makes plans with you then leaves you hanging as if your time doesn't matter. He is always late or cancels at the last minute and he may not even text you to let you know. The Flake can't be counted on for anything. The Flake will make plans to do things with you and never follow through. This jerk often seems to have schedule conflicts, stomach issues and forgets stuff. He will either come up with some lame excuse for not showing up or not show up at all. But then, he may never have intended to meet up with you in the first place. His absence may not matter much, but waiting around for him to show up gets old quick. If your new bar buddy doesn't show up and leaves you to hang out by yourself then he is probably a Flake.

If you see a pattern to his behavior then he is either a passive person and is afraid to disappoint you up front or he is so popular he overbooks his free time. Or, he just may not be into you but feels obligated to hang out with you for some reason. This jerk may be dealing with depression or some form of social anxiety. So try not to let this jerk make you feel bad about yourself or wonder what you did to make him ditch at the last moment.

If you try to create an intimate relationship with a Flake you will be very disappointed. It's difficult to build a relationship with a Flake because he is so unreliable and often leaves you hanging. This jerk makes you feel like you always come last. There are limits to how many times you will put energy into making futile plans before you give up and quit. And that may be just what he wants anyway because that is how he acts.

FLAMING PANTS LIAR

This jerk likes to take you on a journey into a world of fiction where he is the creator, the master, and the god. It's his domain and he will suck you into it every time he opens his mouth. This jerk could not tell the truth if his life depended on it. He is a habitual liar and he enjoys watching you slide deeper and deeper into his pit of misleading statements. If it's not a lie about his past then it's a lie about his made up friends. He lies about everything and he is really good at excuses. It's almost like he carries them around in his head like a stack of get out of trouble free cards. If you catch him off guard his default setting is 'I forgot', or 'I was too busy', 'I lost my phone', or 'my brother needs me to babysit his pet tiger for the weekend'. This jerk can't just tell you that he is a little low on cash this weekend, he has to lie about it. This jerk gets a high out of lying to you. He is running on a power trip thinking that if he can sound important then you will think he is important.

The part that makes this jerk a jerk is that you are investing your time and efforts to get to know him and he is cheating you out of the truth. It would be a lot easier to invest your time in a romance novel than to accommodate his disrespectful games of rearranging plans, waiting for him to show up or call, wondering if his make-believe friends and family are okay, and listening to his endless and meaning-less blabberings.

GOOD OL' BOY

This good-natured home mechanic often drives a rusty muscle car or pickup. He generally speaks with a country accent or drawl. He likes gun collecting, carries one knife in his pocket and another in his boot. He likes to get together with his buddies and watch football or hunt and fish. He only listens to country or hard rock music and likes to drink cheap beer. He's not generally a bad person but does come off at times to be a little racist because he enjoys a racist joke here and there, but really couldn't care less about a person's race or religion. He's always out for a good time such as fast driving and a few bar fights now and then. This jerk is country to the bone, hard working and prefers a simple life.

This blue-collar, stock car loving country boy likes to think he knows-it-all and can be difficult to deal with at times, especially in arguments. He has a tendency to be unreasonably stubborn, unyielding and downright bull-headed.

He would rather hang out with the boys tinkering with pickup trucks than do anything meaningful with you. He never has time for you but time for his good ol' boy network. He treats you like he would treat his lawn mower, if not needed put it away and take it out again when he is ready to use it. He is always sending mixed messages about the way he feels about you. He will generally talk with you about anything and everything external but is unwilling to talk about how he feels or understand how you feel.

He shows up or calls when he wants to. This egotistical jerk is testing to see how much bad behavior you will tolerate. This jerk neglects you on purpose to keep your mind focused on him. He ignores you hoping you will try really hard to get noticed again, and thus go above and beyond to please him. He really does test you to put forth all your efforts to keep the relationship going. If you want to understand him better get him a dog and watch how he treats it. He will likely treat you the same way.

HEAT SEEKER

Have you ever had a dog or a cat that just liked to be next to you? This jerk is just like that. His personal space is very small and he wants to include you in it. If he isn't touching you he is trying too. This jerk stands unnecessarily close and when he talks to you he puts his blabbering mouth really close to your face. He follows you around so close that whenever you change direction you bump into him or step on his foot.

He has no sense of personal space and is unaffected by hints that he is too close. This jerk acts like he is emotionally needy. His close proximity demands your attention. He is clingy and annoying and he doesn't like being left alone. He lacks respect for your boundaries and needs to constantly touch you all the time. It's like he never gets enough attention. This jerk will bug you to no end.

Closeness can be nice and comforting at times but this jerk needs it all the time. He may just need more attention than you are willing to give. So unless you are the touchy-feely kind of person yourself, the best thing you can do is act like you just don't see or hear him and walk away, act like he simply disappeared into thin air and don't stop walking until you find another empty barstool three blocks away.

HERO

When it comes to relationship problems, this jerk is usually the first responder at the bar. He wastes no time in spotting possible prospects for his little dramatic play. Heroes are attracted to vulnerable women with emotional issues or those who have a history of abuse, trauma or addictions. He often over glamorizes these women as damsels in distress and it's up to him to save them.

The Hero makes it his duty to help these women through whatever it is they are dealing with. Then he will try to maintain a relationship with them regardless of how codependent and dysfunctional it may become even when he knows he is just being used. He will defend her destructive behaviors even if they are harmful to himself.

This Jerk seeks out these kinds of relationships because they provide him with a sense of indispensability and significance. He engineers situations through these relationships where he is needed. He wants an opportunity to rescue someone and be the center of attention. He loves being that person she cannot possibly do without. He ensures that she becomes dependent on him by trying to control every aspect of the relationship. He takes someone with low self-esteem and crushes whatever power she has left. He does nothing to empower her or to actually help her at all. He's an unfortunate romantic compensating for a lack of affection with a craving for valor. This Hero will never be able to save himself and he may actually be the one in grave peril. So if you need help, tell him you would rather wait for Superman.

INVISIBLE MAN

Now you see him, now you don't. This jerk performs a little magic trick where he disappears for a month (or more) and then reappears, miraculously remembering your phone number, playing dumb or claiming amnesia. He is prepared to do whatever it takes to pick up the relationship again. But he didn't care that his sudden departure caused you to worry about him. Perhaps even wonder if it was something you did to cause him to disappear. He expects to just come back gingerly with lame excuses, but the bottom line is that there is no excuse. If nothing else, you at least deserved a 'see ya next month, bye'.

The truth is, he probably met someone and took up with her until she got tired of his feeble-minded antics and dumped him for a new toy leaving him out in the cold. So after an interlude of prowling, he realized you were better than what he is able to find or all he has left.

This jerk disrespects you coming and going. First by vanishing without a trace and again by assuming you'll just pick up where you left off and take him back. If you do take him back you may want to have him wear a false nose, a pair of goggles, some bandage wraps, a long coat, and shoes so you can be sure

David Dasnod

that he hasn't vanished on you again.

JERKPIRE

If you happen to be sitting at a bar you may not notice this jerk materialize. This seducer preys on the insecurity of passive victims. He acts without moral restraint, defies convention and likes to projects himself as a free thinker. The Jerkpire is the prince of nightclubs, the hypnotist of your will. The egotistical forces that sustain this jerk are beyond comprehension. His heightened sense of self enhances his superhuman belief that he is superior to all other mortals.

The Jerkpire subsist by feeding on those things that make you uniquely you. He will demand your allegiance to his beliefs. This jerk misinterprets the word 'No' into the word resistance. His intentions are to suppress your thoughts and replace them with his own. When he looks at you in a mirror he expects to see his own image reflecting back.

He will attempt to draw you away from your principles and corrupt your values. The further he can suck you away from yourself the closer you may become like him and the stronger his powers grow over you. He will try to convince you that you will have to be a jerk to make it in this world. He believes that if he can turn you into a jerk as well then his behavior must be right.

But despite his many powers and skills, he can not step one foot inside your head unless invited, but once allowed to enter your mind he will remain in your thoughts all the time. This jerk is truly an arrogant, suppressive and disrespectful slob disguising himself as a suave, charismatic lover boy. It will take more than a glove of garlic to send this ghoul away so your best not to invite him into your head in the first place.

JOKER

The Joker is the guy at the bar poking pinholes in everyone's plastic cups during last call. He's the jerk that is always entertaining himself at someone else's expense because he loves to draw attention to himself. He seldom misses an opportunity to sling a wisecrack or a witty put-down at someone. He takes pride in his sadistic sense of humor and he actually believes he is funny and won't understand if you don't think so too.

The upside to The Joker is that he tends to be in a good mood and that alone is refreshing where most crowds are concerned and his mood does encourage others to lighten up. In small doses, his humor may liven up the lamest of parties. However, he seldom balances his sadistic humor with prudence or restraint. His little pranks and playful tricks are intended to put you in an embarrassing situation. His humor is often inappropriate and may come off at times as offensive. He is impulsive, often blurting out witty comments about your looks or the way you talk. He is unable to resist pulling pranks on you without giving it any thought. He will poke fun at you by making faces or gestures behind your back. He is the guy that interrupts you while are trying to talk with a friend just for the fun of it. This jerk messes with you a lot and may even tell white lies about you as a practical joke.

The Joker pulls pranks, lies, and jokes around in order to feel dominant and liked by others. It gives his ego a boost to make someone suffer, even if it's only just a little. His insecurity keeps him from instantly escalating his pranks to a higher level; so he builds up to it, slowly testing with each jab to see if it is safe to take it up a notch. So he will poke at you and jab you with his witty puns and comments as long as he feels it is safe. His sadistic sense of humor will continue to escalate as long as you allow him to enjoy his antics. A good way to get this jerk to buzz off is to get a heavy-set friend to lean against him and squish him against the bar like the pesky insect he is.

JOHNNY APPLESEED

The Johnny Appleseed jerk is usually a drifter and like most other jerks, spreads his seed far and wide across a large geographical area. He spreads his seeds randomly everywhere he goes. In fact, he may impregnate a whole community before moving on. He is so proficient at this that he has honed it into a craft. There are nurseries filled with his offspring everywhere.

So if you happen to have had a run in with this jerk, don't be worried about not seeing him again because he usually has a circuit and will return again to check in on his old orchards and check out the new breeding stock every year or two.

LABELER

This is the jerk who thinks he is Freud himself. He is all about fixing what isn't broken. He spends all his time reading the latest psychology magazines instead of actually learning anything about being human hands on. He puts a big label on you after one night of conversation and tries his best to convince you that it is you that has the problems.

He's the guy who sits there watching you, with that stupid smug "I knew it" look on his face. He's clearly thinking that by putting a label on you, he has you all figured out and knows just what to do to fix you. He looks at you as if you were some broken piece of pottery he's going to glue back together.

What's sad is that he can't figure out why he has been alone all his life and why no-one actually likes him. He's a boundary stomper and sacrifices the mental well being of anyone he meets to reinforce his own feeble sense of significance. He hasn't got a clue as to what's behind his own pathetic problems so how is he going to fix you?

LEECH

You may have met this jerk in college and here he is again. And yes, he is still the loser parasite you use to know. Chances are he forgot his wallet again and may ask you to pay his bar tab. The Leech pretends to be your friend but he isn't a friend, he's a leech. He latches onto any good-hearted person who is caring and perhaps a little naive to mooch off of. He's the jerk that lives off his so-called friends and has never contributed anything for rent and utilities or even groceries. When he has gotten what he wanted he will detach from his host without a second thought; leaving his host feeling like a patsy.

This is the jerk that begs you to go out with him and when you do, he asks you to go halves on the cost and then he tops that by coming up with some lame excuse as to why he can't pay for his dinner, the movie or condoms.

Don't let this Leech latch on to you because despite all your efforts to make him go away he will cling to you and suck the fun right out of your life without so much as a simple 'Thank you'. If you refuse to go out with him he will be okay, after all, he is likely still living at home with his parents and is sucking the life out of them instead. So, if you do ever find yourself out with one of these jerks, enjoy your evening but be sure to sneak out when the check comes or you"ll be paying for two.

KNOW-IT-ALL

If you ever wanted to know anything at the drop of a hat you will want to keep this jerk around. This jerk will almost bore you with his vast collection of information and gossip, most of which he composes as he goes. This walking and talking encyclopedia likes to impress you with his intellect and will barge in on any conversation you may have with your friends. He is quick to interrupt and correct you with his own content on the subject. He will treat you like your an idiot for not knowing something or act like difficult subjects are obvious.

The Know-it-all is extremely insecure and seeks significance by trying to come off as an expert at everything. He gains a sense of significance if he can finish your sentences, shoot in that word that hangs on your tongue, or take over the subject and dominate the entire conversation completely. He is one of the most oppressing jerks of all. He is highly opinionated, arrogant and literally believes he knows it all!

When this jerk starts to dominate the conversation, you can stop trying to discuss anything of interest to your friends. Don't even waste your breath because nothing you say has any value to him. By the time the bartender shouts 'Last Call', you will know everything about this jerk's high school sports career, but he hasn't asked you a single question about yourself.

This jerk isn't looking for a conversation; he's looking for a sounding board. You can wait around for him to tire of talking or you can shift your attention elsewhere. But If you can hold onto your sense of humor you can use this jerk for entertainment by seeing how long he will go before he wears himself out by yakking his head off about stuff he doesn't know anything about; meanwhile letting him buy all the drinks for you and all your friends. But whatever you do, don't take this jerk seriously, and don't let him get under your skin. Getting upset with him will only add to his sense of significance. It's no wonder that most people avoid this jerk if possible.

MAMA'S BOY

The Mama's Boy will be the man sitting at the bar talking on the phone with his mother asking her if he can stay at the bar a little longer in his wittle-kid voice. She is probably at home washing his underwear as they speak. He's a spoiled little boy in a man's body. His mother may even be paying for the phone he is using to text her on. Hell, she may even be paying for his beer.

Nothing in this jerks life happens that isn't monitored by his mother. She may even be asking by now if she should come and get him because he sounds a little intoxicated. When he hangs up the phone she will probably be calling again before he can set it down. She is as bad as an ex-girlfriend only he won't hang up on her. She won't think you are good enough for him anyway, even if you did want to get involved with this wimpy jerk. She will want to know everything that's going on with you two, and he will be the first to tell her. If you like being the third wheel in a relationship then go ahead and get involved with this jerk.

His mother is the standard that he will measure you by and he will expect you to be just like her. But you will never measure up; that's not how his mother does it. This jerk has some major mommy issues and if he does take to you he will want you to mommy him too.

Even if the Mama's Boy has his own place he will be over at his mommy's house every day. He can't do his own laundry, he doesn't know how to wash dishes and boiling hot dogs is about the extent of his culinary skills. If his apartment is clean, his mother may be the one that keeps it that way. If she can't be there to tuck him in at night then she will do it over the phone instead.

So if you want to step into this creepy soap opera then be my guest. Expect his mother to try and control your life as well. Your house, your clothes, and your job will have to be mother approved. Don't assume you will have any say so in anything without getting his mother's approval first. And of course, she will always have the final say.

The Mama's Boy will eventually expect you to become like his mother and in every way. He is used to getting his way from his mother and will expect the same from you as well. And god forbid if he should ever get sick, geez! She will practically move in with you.

MAN WHORE

This nasty jerk has no self-respect and uses alcohol as a scapegoat. He is likely to sleep with your sister or mother as well as your friends, daughter and even the toothless girl at the end of the bar. Anyone is up for grabs and having sex with them is justified if alcohol is involved.

He is there to use and to be used by you if that is what you are looking for. He is likely to be in and out of bed with anyone and everyone he encounters. This jerk is addicted to sex and may have other addictions as well. Save yourself the heartbreak and headache by staying out of a meaningful relationship with this disposable jerk. He is the type that will cheat on you without a second thought.

The man whore is always looking for a new sex partner and he is likely to pass on to you a few creepy crawlies as well. His thirst for sex is an obsession. Sex takes priority over everything including his job, his home, and finances. His order of things that are important goes like this, sex, more sex, a little boozing, sex and then whatever it takes to get more sex. Don't confuse this jerk's addiction with a passion though. The Man Whore is too undisciplined and unmotivated to do anything worthwhile to be

David Dasnod

driven by a passion.

MR. GADGET

You may find Mr. Gadget sitting at a bar playing with the latest app on his phone, oblivious to the beer chugging, joke telling and redneck brawls going on around him. Be it collections or the latest electronic gizmo, this jerk always finds something inanimate to nurture, cuttle and tend to.

Mr. Gadget uses all his gadgetry to conveniently avoid intimate interactions. He spends more time with his gadgets than he does with people. He uses gadgets as a way of escaping from feelings of guilt, anxiety, depression or helplessness and by doing so he jeopardizes significant relationships, his job, and future career opportunities.

If he isn't playing with his gadgets he is thinking about them. He has found that if he appears preoccupied he can remain uninvolved in the affairs of others. When he isn't able to be with his toys he becomes moody or irritable and will eventually become depressed. But he won't allocate any time for other activities outside the range of his gadgetry. So unless you are a Miss Gadget yourself this jerk would rather play with his gadget than you.

NAMBY-PAMBY

This wimpy little pipsqueak has such a big ouchie for such a little jerk. This weakling is often small in stature or tall and skinny. He doesn't play well with others and uses victim dramas as a puzzling form of manipulation. The Namby-Pamby is a self-centered goofball that has a tendency to sabotage his own underhanded schemes by acting like a jerk doing it. He lacks consideration and empathy towards others to make his victim dramas work for him. He's rude, selfish, emotionally undeveloped and immature. This complainer really is a useless, spoiled, baby-man. He is attracted to childish things and will likely spend most of his time playing video games. He lives in a fantasy world and may even believe his game adventures are real.

This jerk plays the victim because he really is a victim of his own making. He can't understand that people have to earn a living in order to fulfill their needs and be free from financial restraints. This jerk is dependent on others for the things he needs in order to stay in his fantasy world. He uses his victim dramas hoping to trigger a sympathetic response in others and then exploit them for everything he can get.

This jerk is able to keep a job but won't. He is quick to find fault with it and expects to get paid to just stand around. He's always upset that the world doesn't just give him whatever wants. He holds the world responsible for his unhappiness. He always makes a big show of suffering. Life is so unfair... I shouldn't have to do anything I don't want to... blah blah blah... on and on and on. It makes you wonder if he ever left home. He probably still lives with his mom and dad.

The Namby-Pamby refuses to grow up and there is a good chance he never will as long as he can stay tethered to a few sympathetic accommodators. So go ahead and buy this jerk a drink if you want but don't be surprised if he starts in with his request for acquisitions. This jerk is pathetic and should be left alone to sit in his soggy diapers along with his boo-boos.

NEGATIVE THINKER

It may be a beautiful day. Your thoughts may be pleasantly positive, lifting you to new heights of inspiration. A fresh zest for life begins to grow within you, and then this cloud comes along and sets up camp right over your beer and barstool.

This human sinkhole is so depressing he can suck the smile off of a clown. Thinking the worst and dragging you into his suck-pit of despair, he almost makes you want to trade in your beer for a good stiff whiskey.

It is easy to recognize him in a bar because there will be a five-foot void that surrounds him. Nobody is anywhere near him. It's almost like he is sitting in his own little bubble of isolation. It would be advisable to avoid this jerk as well. There is little hope of cheering him up and if you do he will find something wrong with being cheerful.

His world is twisted with a strange sense of logic that goes something like this. If he expects the worst, then he won't be disappointed if it happens. In other words, he feels better to be proved right with his negative prediction than to induce good things to happen and be disappointed if it doesn't happen. His negative thinking has become a habit of thought. He has become hopeless. And to him, being hopeless is a safe place to be because it has become comfortable and undisapointing.

This pessimist lives in a lights-on lights-off world, an all or nothing, a black and white painted pit. He won't consider the subtle shades of gray to be an option. And if he did consider the shades of gray worthy of his graces he would be too critical of them. Such as, if a bartender slid him a drink down the bar it wouldn't be straight enough; where you or I wouldn't care. 'Hey, I got a beer!'

Besides, there are better ways to spend your time here on earth than being exposed to this pickle-puss. So when you do meet this black hole of despair stay out of his gravitational pull. And if he does try to suck you in just hit your warp speed button and put about twenty light years between you and him.

NICE GUY

You may be thinking, 'Nice Guys can be jerks?'. Jerks manipulate. They don't negotiate. Nice Guys have trouble communicating what they want so they try to manipulate others in a passive way by being super gentle, compassionate, sensitive and vulnerable. And who in their right mind wouldn't want to have a relationship with someone like that? He puts the needs of others before his own, avoids confrontations, will do anything for you, gives emotional support and tries to stay out of trouble. Wow, what a Nice Guy. But wait! He is usually honest, loyal, courteous and respectful too. I'm impressed, buy that jerk a drink.

Genuine Jerks will let a woman know in his own way that he's interested in her. Genuine jerks are not passive, they tend to be very assertive, to say the least. A Nice Guy will tippy-toe around and come off as being unassertive by not expressing his true feelings. He knows he's unattractive and boring. It's no wonder he lacks confidence as well. So because this jerk lacks the confidence, the looks, and the personality, the Nice Guy will attempt to approach a woman in an uninteresting, mild-mannered way. He will try to develop a friendship with her in hopes that she will eventually fall madly in love with him. This jerk will seldom let her know he is interested in her sexually. Instead, he will silently hope to eventually turn the friendship into a sex feast.

This pathetic jerk opens himself up to be used in any way she chooses. He thinks he can win her over with servitude. The Nice Guy can easily be manipulated into cleaning his new friend's apartment, walk her dog, run her errands or anything else including listening to her talk about her dates with other men just to be with her. The nice guy behaves like a friendly doormat and lacks the sex appeal required for an intimate relationship and no girl wants to go to bed with a doormat.

PLAYER

The Player is the perfect example of a noncommittal jerk. This guy is up for any game in town. It's easy for him to enter into a conversation game because he has nothing invested and nothing to lose. And the winnings just keep pouring in. He can strum on you like a well-tuned guitar while placing all his bets on his next winning catchphrase.

The only thing the Player wants out of the game is the adventure it provides him. He is addicted to the sensation of conquest and thus the reaffirmation of significance. The charisma of the Player radiates from his " I'm Winning" attitude, it's appealing and he knows it. He may make you feel like you're the only person in his life, and you may be for the moment. At least until his attention wanders elsewhere. But because the Player is shallow and lacks any real personality he quickly becomes boring and you may soon find your own attention wandering elsewhere as well.

POMPOUS PUFFER FISH

This jerk is all about feeling superior. He puffs himself up to look better than he really is, but he is only full of hot air. The Pompous Puffer Fish is very insecure, so as a way to protect his fragile ego he will come off as being arrogant and disrespectful. He seeks comfort in feeling that he is better than everybody else. His mouth is filled with a razor-sharp tongue that can shred anyone into tattered pieces. He acts as if he is angered by something and tends to be snappy. He's afraid of other jerks in his territory and will quickly grow to hate jerks of his own kind. It may be interesting to see his response to seeing himself in a mirror.

This cold-blooded vertebrate is unable to smile because smiles are for warm-blooded creatures. If you spend enough time in a bar with this jerk, you will likely be exposed to a lethal dose of his poisonous personality. You may lose your ability to smile and to laugh. His poisonous attitude will paralyze your happy mood and destroy any hopes of having a good time. But the damage isn't irreversible. Just have a bouncer toss him out to dry in the parking lot and party away. You'll feel stronger and happier with each second away from him you get.

POOR BOY

This could be your typical college student or perhaps just a pitiful, lazy jerk that is too good to earn his own keep. This vagabond is like a stray dog in that he only hangs around for scraps and free drinks. He either doesn't know how to save his money or he doesn't make enough of it to pay his expenses. He never has any money but is humble enough to be grateful for anything you do happen to share with him.

He either gets his clothes for free or shops for them exclusively at thrift stores. You may see him standing in line at the soup kitchen or being arrested for vagrancy. But being poor isn't what makes this jerk a jerk. He's a jerk because he makes poverty his way of life. He could get a job if he wanted, or he could even start his own business if he desired. He could make a living for himself but he lacks the discipline to do things he doesn't want to do. He may get a job but he doesn't stay at it long. So until he learns to practice self-control he will forever be a snowflake in the sandstorm of life, his destruction is inevitable, regardless of how much you try to help him.

PRINCE

The Prince is a self-proclaimed monarch of the bar who ranks himself above everyone else including the bartender. This noble Prince of booze is the most distinguished drunk in his kingdom. He is used to getting by on his looks and believes it's his right to treat other people shabbily. He has always been coddled, pampered and spoiled. He has been treated with excessive indulgence from his earliest childhood. He has no concept of hard work or having to struggle to make a living. This snob lacks consideration for others and has developed an undeserved sense of entitlement. Only the best liquor and the finest maidens will do for his fluctuating harem.

This vain Adonis is a true lover of himself. The Prince is conceited, egoistic and narcissistic. He spends a lot of time on his looks. He doesn't miss an opportunity to pose in front of any reflective surface to adore his bulging muscles and rippling abs or his thick wavy hair and meticulously trimmed face. It's enough to make you feel like the third wheel if you find yourself in a relationship with him.

Unless you yourself are a princess of his kind you may want to save yourself the trouble of hoping for anything meaningful to happen between you and his Lordship. The only long-term relationship he wants is the one he has with himself.

Beware and admire this jerk from a distance. Unless you are the finest thing that ever walked the planet yourself, he will never compliment you on how nice you look or even notice if you have gained or lost any weight. This guy is in a perpetual pageant and will likely spend more on his cosmetics in a week than you ever will. So if you like to feel beautiful while out having fun, send The Prince and his entourage into exile.

SILENT CLAM

This jerk won't speak to you. Why? I don't know, he won't say. He is just there. Tight-lipped, floating about on the currents of conversations listening, watching and pretending he is part of the group. The Silent Clam is easy to find in a bar, you just dig around until you find someone that doesn't respond to you well verbally. He usually just looks at you like a goldfish in a fish tank. This social mollusk hides inside a hard shell of solitude and is very difficult to open up with small talk.

His quiet presence may make you uncomfortable not knowing what he is thinking; rather he is a friend or foe; if he is judging you or just shy. Maybe, like other invertebrates, he just doesn't have anything to say.

Personally, I believe this jerk is an alien from outer space placed here to spy on us in order to launch an invasion. Whatever he is planning it sure isn't to discuss anything with us. So until we know more about this guy it may be best to be discrete in his presence. If he wants to follow you around like a clump of mud, eavesdropping in on every word you speak then maybe it's time to practice a second language with your friends.

SPEEDY BOY

This jerk will likely ask you to bring along your luggage and belongings on your first date because about halfway through the date he will want you to move in with him. This jerk becomes infatuated easily which makes him addicted to relationships. He will be in and out of your life so fast he will leave you shaking your head wondering what just happened.

His feelings for you are superficial and it doesn't take a lot to make him feel connected to you. He quickly becomes enamored with you and thinks it's love at first sight. He likes the feeling when someone makes him feel special but he doesn't realize that he is actually addicted to the chemical reactions taking place in his brain when he becomes infatuated. He feels the intense romantic attraction to you, everything feels fresh and exciting and all he wants to do is be with you. The feelings are passionate and spontaneous. His mind is emotionally captivated and it's okay because nothing else matters to him.

But it's only temporary. His neediness begins to drain you and you feel tired all the time. You're exhausted and the thought of spending another moment with him begins to make your brain cringe.

What was cute about him is now annoying. The things you did together that you thought was sexy and energizing have become routine and somewhat repulsive.

He feels your attempts to pull away from him and begins to feel the chemical withdraws. He becomes resentful and moody. You no longer do it for him. He is losing his infatuation with you and he begins searching for someone new. Someone to get his chemistry moving again. This jerk is enthralled to his emotional highs and the obsessive sexual activities that go along with being stoned on infatuation.

SPORTS ENTHUSIAST

This jerk isn't hard to spot because he is covered with sports team logos. They are on his key chain, his wallet, and even his socks. This guy is obsessed with sports. He will usually be in a playful argument with someone that supports a lesser team than his. He will be grunting with his cave buddies and over-dramatize his high-fives as if the highest high-five wins some honorable place in the tribe.

This guy lives to know the latest sports trivia as it happens twenty-four hours a day, seven days a week. I agree that a person has to have a passion, but sports is his obsession. This jerk is all about sports. He has to watch every game of the season and gets depressed when his team loses.

The Sports Enthusiast jerk is addicted to sports. He may spend money and invest time in this obsession that may be better off spent on other aspects of his life. His relationships and work may be suffering because of it. He spends all his time focused on the scoreboards and less time on those things that really matter. He may come out of his trance someday and find that his children have grown up and moved away and that his wife left for a better life five years ago.

He might spend some time with you to earn a few 'score' points but when his sports is on you know where you can find him. He isn't going to get involved in what you want to do because he is preoccupied with his games but he will want you to run out and get more munchies and drinks while he remains glued to the TV for hours upon hours.

If you really love sports he's the guy for you. But the Sports Enthusiast won't care that the house needs to be painted, that the cat hasn't been fed in four days or that you haven't gone out for dinner once in the last three months. All he cares about is his TV, his beer, snacks, and his sports channel.

SUCTION CUP

This Jerk floats around looking for anyone to attach himself too. He likes to talk non-stop about things that may only matter to himself. Any attentive action on your part is enough to send his tentacles around you demanding your full undivided attention. If you do get a chance to focus on someone else, he just sits there as if to pick up where he left off or will likely do anything to place himself back onto center stage, even if it means embarrassing you by being overly dramatic at times. If he should happen to attach himself to you, you will almost have to sneak out the bathroom window to get away from him.

This jerk isn't interested in you as a person or else he would let the conversation flow both ways. The Suction Cup seems to be more stuck on himself than you but he wants all your attention. This jerk is not only clingy but has some strange entitlement issues. He will eventually become whiny and start complaining as well. You can see why he is floating around the bar alone; he's almost creepy.

His demands on your attention is almost painful and will go into a feeding frenzy sucking up all your attention if allowed. He needs to manipulate you into giving him your attention and once he finds what works on you he will graciously suck you dry.

TAILGATER

The Tailgater will pop up close behind you in a crowd and follow you around until he loses his fascination with you. This annoying jerk does not understand the meaning of personal space and will pull up in hot pursuit right behind you. You may be at risk of being rear-ending or end up with his drink on your back if you stop too quick. He clings to your personal bubble so close people may soon start to think he is your submissive plaything.

It's hard to tell what's going on in his head but I'm sure it entails a fantasy involving you glancing over your shoulder at him. If he thinks you are onto him he will quickly veer off in another direction in order to avoid an intimate collision. But don't be surprised if you should happen to find yourself under surveillance from across the room. This guy is just plain weird.

TASKMASTER

This jerk is organized and methodical when it comes to getting what he wants. Although this guy is quiet and reserved he is a master at needling and conditioning you into his little slave. If you give in to his logical excuses and reasoning for doing things for him you will eventually forfeit your freedom to act upon your own thoughts and feelings. This jerk wears you down by constantly correcting your every action, slowly trapping you in a pen of expectations.

By suppressing your feelings and spontaneity you may soon find yourself mentally locked in his servitude. This jerk creates an unspoken book of rules for you to follow and is often obsessed with doing things 'by that book'. His own security is very important to him, which gives him an air of seriousness and inflexibility. This jerk enjoys placing himself in a position of authority over you. He demands a lot from you, yet takes your efforts to please him for granted. There is no end to the petty rules and expectations. This jerk expects a life of leisure and comfort even if it requires you to take on a second or third job.

TYPICAL JERK

The typical jerk likes it when people react to him. He likes the sense of significance reactions provide. Feeling significant is like a drug to this jerk and over time, he can grow addicted to this feeling. He won't allow himself to care about anyone, not even himself, so he displaces the feelings of significance as a substitute for affection. Wanting to feel love subconsciously and settling for significance leaves the typical jerk feeling dissatisfied and in a state of restless emotional discomfort.

To the typical jerk, his significance is reinforced by getting others to express such reactions as awe, respect, admiration, attention, or fear. To him, any action that stimulates these reactions is justified because he feels entitled to his significance at the expense of others. This jerk feels entitled to whatever he can extract from you and expects a lot more. And despite all that you give him he will always feel that he should be getting more from you than he does. But regardless of what you give this jerk, he will always bear resentment towards you because you either didn't give him what he wanted or you didn't give him enough of it. This resentment festers from the fact that you have it, he doesn't and he feels entitled to it all.

When you are giving him what he wants you are useful and valuable but you are never more than just an accommodator. The jerk only sees you for your usefulness and that is all he will ever see in you. If you cease to be useful he will try to manipulate you into his service again, and again, or he will simply replace you. He will never feel anything towards you because if he did you would no longer be replaceable and that would give you power over him. The best you can hope for from this jerk is to be over-valued. This makes any meaningful long-term relationship with the Typical Jerk impossible. The best you can get from any jerk is an arrangement. A relationship based on contingencies and conditions, potentially developing into a dysfunctional relationship over time at best.

WALKING BAND-AID

This jerk's persona is soft-hearted, kind and sensitive. He acts as if he cares by listening to you rant and rave about your troubles. He'll hold you and comfort you with words of reassurance. He is there for you any time of the day or night. But it's all just a deception. He doesn't really care about you. He wants to attend to you because it makes him feel he has value. Once he senses that he has become valuable and therefore significant in your eyes, he will feel entitled to your affection. To him, being significant to someone is equal to being loved by them.

It actually causes him emotional stress if you refuse his help. He doesn't understand why you would refuse to let him help you. But he isn't concerned with empowering you, on the contrary, he wants you to conform to his expectations. He wants to transform you into his conception of something ideal.

Like most things this situation will get worse before it gets better. This jerk is expecting you to surrender yourself to him because he feels he has earned your affection. Refusing to do so would be like telling him that he hasn't done enough for you yet. It will confuse him and frustrate him. He may become violent and vengeful. His expectations are unjustified but over time he will feel he owns you and all your affection. He will try using guilt and shame in order to get you to surrender to him. He will criticize you and try to convince you that you will be lost without him. He is likely to try every means of manipulation there is to get you to surrender to him. So, it may sting at first, but the best thing you can do is rip this Walking Band-Aid off of you and get as far away from him as you can.

WILD MAN

The wild man has an adventuresome spirit and he thrives on just being alive. He is not much on following social rules because he likes to believe he is free to do his own thing. His sense of adventure and desire for constant action may cause him to become bored rather quickly. He may have a circle of friends but he is mainly a loner; forlorn and abandoned; a cultural orphan. To him, relationships like everything else need to be adaptable and spontaneous. He is like a wild animal responding only to the world before him. He is not concerned with how he affects others and may exhibit outbursts of anger if things don't go his way.

This jerk remains detached in relationships and does not respond well emotionally in intimate settings. His range of expressions is limited due to his lack of social exposure. He does not desire close relationships and will always choose activities where he does not have to interact much with others. So if you should happen to wonder upon this jerk accidentally don't take it personally if you can't hold his attention for very long, because unless it is mating season he may not pay too much attention to you.

WRANGLER

This cowboy generally has a good-natured, easy-going attitude mixed with a good sense of humor and will more than likely drive a pickup truck. His outlook is 'every day is going to be another great day' and sets out to make it so. Although he has a rugged appearance the Wrangler is usually an urban, heterosexual male with an interest in fashion and a refined sense of taste in art, music, and literature. He will be clean-shaved, wears clean clothes and will have more teeth than tattoos. He doesn't curse much nor does he spit tobacco or drink too much. You can always tell if you are in close proximity of a Wrangler because the sound of boot heels on the bar floor will give him away.

However, on the ornery side, this jerk finds cute wild mustangs the most interesting for breaking in. He is adept at saddling young mares that have had little experience in dating and possesses a pleasant disposition. But If he can't find any open range strays he will try to rustle another guy's girl by cutting her from the herd and rounding her up with com-pliments and false promises. When things start to get serious he assumes he has finally got her saddle broke and is off rounding up another stud mare to break in.

The Wrangler is effective at setting up the post-sex breakup to fall in his favor by leading his fancy to believe he is a sensitive guy early on. That way when he is ready to put her out to pasture it will be easier to coax her in again by making the whole thing look like it's her fault for coming on too strong, and consequently, she will take him back if he chooses to return for another ride in the saddle.

THE ABUSER
JERK TYPE

An abusive jerk directs abusive behaviors at his victim for the purpose of manipulating her. To him, abuse is geared towards the desired outcome. This jerk uses abuse to get you to react to him in such a way as to make it easier for him to manipulate you.

Your first reaction to abuse is defense. When you become defensive you become reactive to the actions of your abusers. The abusive jerk can only manipulate you if he can get you to react to his behaviors. This is the first thing we all learn as babies when we cry and wine to get our needs met. After a while, our caregivers stop paying attention to our whining and crying so we become abusive to get their attention. So you can see just how far this jerk has developed beyond the crib. Over the years he has become skillful at manipulation through abuse but the intention is basically the same, only the diaper is bigger.

This jerk derives pleasure from overpowering someone at a disadvantage; it makes him feel powerful. He is a bully. He doesn't respect people who are shy. This jerk only respects what he fears and shy people do not pose much of a threat to anyone. He has little respect for anyone unless they have some form of power over him.

This is the jerk that is rude to cashiers and will eventually become unpleasant towards you as well. He can be very impersonal, arrogant, mean or abrasive. He is condescending and demeaning. He humiliates or embarrasses you with little to no concern towards your feelings. He does not respect your values or boundaries. He feels entitled to go through your stuff, mock you when you are upset and refused to take no for an answer and will quickly resort to physical force to get you to comply with his wishes.

An abusive jerk often slaps, kicks and or punches you when he is upset. He will hurt you on purpose by twisting your arm or pulling your hair. He will try to upset you by destroying your stuff and saying things to hurt you. His abusive behaviors can do long-lasting mental harm to you. Even years after having this jerk in your life, the experience may leave you in a reflective daze trying to make sense of it all.

The abusive jerk may use many forms of abuse to manipulate you into doing what he wants. An overt abuser is an obvious abuser, imposing verbal, physical, sexual and or emotional abuse on you. An overt abuser mainly uses physical threats and intimidation through violence to manipulate his victim. An overt abuser's behavior is indisputable and easily observable whereas a covert abuser is driven by a need to assert and maintain ambiguous control over you. The covert abuser gets into your mind and ultimately controls you through psychological manipulation. The covert abuser creates an atmosphere of fear, intimidation, instability, and unpredictability. In a pure covert abusive relationship, there are little if any acts of physical abuse.

The abusive jerk splatters abuse on everyone around him all the time. His abusive conduct is the only way he knows how to react to a world he views as being hostile and exploitative. He acts as though his behavior is "hard-wired" into his very being. It is who he has become, who he is and what he does. The abusive jerk is explosive and impulsive. He has little control over his anger. He responds to injuries to his ego, conflicting ideas or beliefs with rage. Some abusive jerks only target one person repeatedly and viciously. While others do not discriminate in choosing their prey. An abusive jerk may have a history of assault or other disrespectful behaviors. He carries around his pent-up frustrations which makes him confrontational and explosive with a terrible temper when under stress. The Abusive Jerk Types should really be avoided if possible.

ANGRY JERK

This is the jerk at the bar yelling at the waitress and throwing his drink across the room while asking innocent bystanders what the hell they are looking at. He's a pressure cooker on two legs and no-one knows when he will blow.

He's mad about everything and is often found screaming about all the things he hates about his life, his job, the auto mechanic, politicians, having to say please and thank you and on and on. He's extremely impatient and restless. He's intolerant of delays and gets himself irritated easily if the bartender doesn't notice his drink is empty right away.

When you meet this jerk he usually starts the conversation off by telling you about his conniving ex-wife, and that his boss is a half-wit, that people are idiots and that the bartender doesn't know the difference between a good scotch and the crap he's drinking (I usually found it in my heart to give these jerks the crappy liquors on purpose). He is often rude to the bar staff as well as the clientele. It's enough to make a person wonder what this jerk may have eaten with all those sandwiches and chips he ordered over the years.

The angry jerk is extremely impulsive and his mood is unstable and unpredictable. He is likely to fly off in an angry temper tantrum at a moment's notice. Other self-defeating behaviors like driving too fast because he's mad, or breaking and throwing things during a fit and getting into fights don't make it easy to tolerate being around this jerk.

Developing a relationship with this jerk would be precarious and difficult in the least. He may start off all nice and reassuring that he will never harm you. Just watch how he treats others. The way he treats other people may be the way he will eventually be treating you. So don't ignore the signs. Someday his outburst may be directed towards you.

If this jerk ever grabs your arm in anger or pushes you around, punches the walls or destroys your stuff get away from him. End the relationship as soon as possible. You don't have to lose your dignity but you don't have to be overly polite either. This jerk is verbally as well as physically abusive. Don't feel you have to wait for the first punch to be thrown, to toss in the towel and get out of the ring with this jerk.

BULLY

The Bully is the jerk at the bar harassing the little computer geek by flipping his tie and thumping him on the back of the head when he tries to take a sip from his scotch and water. It's kinda reminiscent of grade school only with a scotch instead of a carton of milk.

The Bully has never grown up. He has remained uncultured, rude, aggressive and immature. He is deliberately hurtful to those he can intimidate. He may shout and swear at the top of his lungs to get his point across. He likes to make offensive jokes at your expense. The Bully often makes fun of you by belittling you in front of others. He is inclined to make threatening gestures or verbal threats to you if you do not do as he wishes and if you stand up to him he is likely to escalate his behavior.

In some cases, it can be hard to discriminate between a regular intoxicated jerk and an intoxicated bully jerk. The average jerk will say and do stupid things without thinking. The conventional jerk is usually careless, thoughtless and tactless, and may even do these things with the intent of hurting you. But The Bully will specifically target you. If allowed he will continue to intimidate and badger you on a regular basis. His harassment is intentional and tends to escalate. He may use physical intimidation, starts rumors about you and teases you to no end. He is likely to do anything to torment you or anyone who is afraid to stand up to him. He takes delight in causing suffering in people who have never done anything but fear him.

This jerk lacks empathy and does not experience compassion, guilt or remorse, so he does not feel bad when he bullies you. So no matter how much you try to understand what this jerk is doing or why he's doing it, it won't make sense to you. This jerk gets a feeling of power by making you nervous or afraid. The Bully feeds on power for its own sake and for the sensation of superiority it gives him. It's a power game and this jerk goes for the throat. His game is simple; to make himself feel good by causing you to feel bad.

To stay out of his game remove your need to prove anything to this jerk. The opinion of this jerk isn't really an opinion but a ploy to get you to play his game. Just remember, your pride heals faster than finding a good dentist.

Try not to attract any undue attention to yourself; but if he does notice you, you may have the sudden urge to crawl in a hole, hide in the restroom or jump out a window. But whatever you decide to do stay calm and hope the storm blows itself out; but take the first available exit you get. Courting the bully's favor may help to diffuse the situation if you become the target of the bully's attention but it's unlikely to help much; unless you are really good at buying drinks for low life jerks.

If you get sucked into his power game you will not get away untouched. It's natural to fear something that may harm you and it's okay to run. Don't waste time arguing with him, get away. If you can't run then do the best you can to protect yourself. You may not be a Kung-fu master, but you can call a good lawyer. In the meantime, a good bouncer will do just fine.

CLAPPERCLAW

This jerk appears kind and helpful on the outside, but under the surface lies the need to sabotage or attack you while appearing innocent. The Clapperclaw's behavior is a form of covert abuse and is very passive aggressive. You may have got a new car recently, or a promotion at work or something that may make the Clapperclaw jealous. You may have said something to him that hurt his feelings or something he simply didn't agree with. He doesn't need much of a reason to make you his next target. This jerk is impossible to deal with because his war with you is a private war for his eyes only. He will never admit that he is on a campaign for your destruction. This jerk is crazy and can make you crazy too.

He will always have someone to vent his hostility upon. He will choose someone safe to victimize that is unable to defend themselves easily; such as a co-worker or neighbor. The Clapperclaw tries to 'get your goat' and wants to see your reactions to his little games. He will try to manipulate you into playing his games so that he can escalate his aggressive assaults against you or get you into trouble. Venting his anger in this way allows him to experience your pain in a sadistic manner. It makes him feel good to see you suffer.

A Clapperclaw will attract people around him that will make excuses for his bad behaviors. This not only makes it easier to deny any wrongdoing when confronted with the evidence but helps him distort the facts. He is great at coming up with excuses but will never admit to doing anything that creates unrest or disorder.

Confronting the Clapperclaw is not very effective. He will either walk away, give you the silent treatment or start yelling at you, becoming very defensive. He can quickly switch over to the victim mode if you do anything to defend yourself against his attacks. The Clapperclaw will want a reason to punish you and will do so in the most unexpected of ways. Just about anything you do to confront him is a waste of time and will only encourage him to continue.

This jerk is angry inside and he has chosen you as his safe little target to displace all that aggression onto. The best thing you can do is document everything no matter how trivial, get a lawyer and start building a lawsuit against him. Chances are when he finds out that you are collecting evidence and talking to a lawyer about him, he will move on to another target and leave you alone. By letting other people know what you intend to do may help him get wind of your intentions and make the attacks stop all that much faster. And hang on to your evidence, it may come in handy; the Clapperclaw may just be circling around for another attack.

CONTROL JERK

All jerks have control issues because jerks manipulate and manipulation is a control tactic. However, there are those jerks that just want to dominate and control others and the Control Jerk is the most prevalent jerk of them all. They are so common that we don't think of them as jerks but as dominating individuals. Well, they are jerks and we would be best off not to forget it so I gave the Control Jerk his own classification.

Unlike the other jerks this insecure jerk is motivated by a deep fear of chaos; of not getting his needs met. The Control Jerk seeks conformity, security, and stability. He is very uncomfortable when things don't fit into his giant box of expectations. That includes what he expects to get from you and when he will get it. Take that and add a pound of paranoia, shake it up and presto; you got a Control Jerk.

He lacks respect for others by dehumanizing them. To him people are things and they only exist to be utilized. This jerk doesn't play well with others nor is he a good candidate for friendship. The Control Jerk will avoid independent people because they are less likely to accommodate him, therefore remain immune to his game. To him, they are unpredictable and disobedient. They can't be manipulated because they don't sacrifice themselves to ease his discomfort and insecurities. Therefore they remain outside the clutches of his approval traps and snares.

But for anyone that is willing to accommodate this jerk, he does not waste any time in taking and maintaining control in the relationship. He wants you to focus on him and his needs. His needs are very important to him and he needs to be sure that someone provides them for him. This makes him over anxious and nervous so everything this jerk does is an attempt to get you to prove to him that there isn't anyone more important to you than him.

He doesn't want you to have fun without him or any outside interests other than those which he totally controls. He will want you to drop your hobbies and any involvement with other people. He questions your loyalty and constantly tests your trustworthiness. He will check up on you and keep track of where you are and who you are with. He will access your computer's history bar and check your phone's dialed numbers right in front of you. This jerk will even notice the bugs on your car's grill and keep track of your mileage to see how far you are driving each day. He will go through your mail, look through your purse, and search through the garbage for evidence of 'unapproved' activities.

If you speak to a member of the opposite sex, you'll

be interrogated about how you know them. He questions why your friends call you, or why you called them and what you talked about. He will wonder why you go to certain places or why it took you so long to run down to the grocery store. He will want to know what you were doing and who you were with. He will even try to catch you in a lie by asking you questions he already knows the answers too. His expectations on you seem unjust. He sets a high standard for you to live by and he will keep you "walking on eggshells". This behavior is designed to manipulate you into becoming dependent on his approval.

Exposure to this jerk is detrimental to your sense of well-being and confidence. As he pulls you away from your friends and family he will gain more and more control over you. When you can no longer take the interrogations you will be screaming and seething. When you are upset his reactions are always logical and cold-hearted. He won't want to listen to your concerns let alone offer you any emotional support. He is enough to make you crazy.

The Control Jerk sees you as his property, something he owns. He becomes intensely possessive of you. He uses your body, demands your time and takes ownership over your things. He dictates to you who you can and can not be with. He will tell you what to wear because he thinks your clothes are too revealing. He may tell you what kind of car to drive, what music to listen to, and how to walk and talk like a real live slave girl.

He is suspicious of your activities and interrogates you constantly. He believes you are seeing someone else when you're not. He gets this way even more when you start to withdraw from him because you no longer want to be around him. But it all comes down to the fact that he doesn't want you to have anything in your life but him. Stay with him and the only thing you will have left in your life is a paranoid man who can't stand having you too far away from him. And that's exactly what this jerk wants because if there isn't anyone else but him in your life then there isn't anyone to hinder his manipulation and dominance over you.

If you want someone that has to know what you are doing and where you are going every minute of every day then this is the jerk of choice. If you don't, then get out while you can. You will end up accommodating his insecurities for the rest of your life. If you do find yourself in a relationship with this jerk and decide to leave him, he will try to make you feel like you are destroying him by leaving. But he will survive without you because he is a jerk, and jerks always find replacements for lost property.

DR. JERKYLL AND MR. CUDDLES

This jerk swings from hateful to lovable and back again in order to condition his target into a weak minded submissive slave. When this jerk is in public he plays Mr. Cuddles, a warm and kind personality; the perfect date. But once he has you alone he transforms into a manipulative creature without compassion or remorse named Jerkyll.

One moment he may be verbally abusive, uttering vulgar obscenities, and threatening you over something petty. The next minute he becomes sweet and kind, calling you pet names and attempts to comfort you. You go through each traumatizing mood change day after day, hoping the never-ending hateful-then-lovable cycle is the last one. He will say offensive and hateful things to you or words designed to chip away at your self-esteem and self-confidence. He always apologizes for his outburst, but the harm is done, precisely as intended.

As time goes by, Dr. Jerkyll's power over you grows stronger and eventually he will not need Mr. Cuddles to sooth over his transgressions. The lack of abuse becomes Mr. Cuddles substitute. You will come to feel like you have no control over his moods, that there is no escaping his abuse. Eventually, you will simply give up and accept your relationship with this unworthy jerk. So before this jerk gets through his first transformation give his beer a sling across the bar and get away from this sociopath. He is evil, self-indulgent and utterly uncaring to anyone but himself regardless of what his other self may tell you.

HEAD MASTER

This jerk is the husband or 'head of the house' who confuses respect for manors. Having manors means you respect yourself enough to be dignified but it doesn't mean you have any respect for others. Just about everything this jerk does is either disrespectful or abusive in one way or another. Most of the time this jerk is either an alcoholic or a religious fanatic (perhaps both). Many fundamental religious husbands fall into this category.

This jerk believes men were put on this earth to boss women around. He actually believes that he is the dominant figure in the relationship and expects you to be submissive to him. If he washes the dishes or helps with the laundry, he makes it a point that he is just helping you do some of your chores.

A romantic relationship with this jerk is far from romantic; it's more like obedience training. He likes to make it known who is the boss. When he yanks your chain he expects you to jump into action. This jerk is likely going to have a list of rules and it isn't important to him that you understand why he makes them but only that you understand that breaking them will result in punishment. He believes he is the self-appointed dictator of the house and lord over all that dwell within.

This jerk has a quick temper and a low tolerance for disobedience. When he gets angry he is likely to become verbally abusive and physically threatening. He believes that if you are afraid of him then you will respect him. You will find yourself honoring his wishes just so he won't get angry again. But he will, he always will; he'll always get angry about something. How else is he going to keep you on your leash?

If you stay in a relationship with this jerk you will eventually give in. Your mind will no longer be able to defend itself. You will conform to his rules because you are afraid not to. You will become obedient and you will get nothing to call your own, except maybe a rubber chew toy and a rug to sleep on.

NARCISSIST

This jerk is easy to spot. He's the guy that brags about himself endlessly. When he talks his monologue is filled with I, my, myself and mine throughout from beginning to end. He depicts himself as intelligent, wealthy, creative and athletic. He will have a lot of photos of himself and his things. This jerk is always talking about his car, all the money he spends, where he has gone, what he has done, his looks and so forth, on and on and on. To him, there isn't anything more important than himself and his stuff and every other aspect of his existence to talk about. This jerk is the king of all jerks. Even jerks can't stand to be around him for very long because he demands so much attention.

This jerk believes that the world was created specifically for him and him alone and that he was the one that created it in all his holiness. Well, maybe not the created by him part but that his world is the only world the whole world and there is nothing but his world so help himself. This jerk is a significance junky and will do anything and I mean anything to obtain a grandiose sense of self-importance. As long as you are a member of his suck-up club he will take you in under his wing, but once you lose your admiration of him he will dispose of you because you are no longer useful to him.

This jerk is very egotistical and wants to believe he is always right regardless of how inflexible and inefficient his ideas are. He does not like to be told he is wrong about anything and will become very defensive. He doesn't like to be around anyone that is more intelligent than he is because he has to work harder to make himself appear superior. He is easily upset and insulted. Any suggested help, advice, or inquiry is seen by this jerk as intentional humiliation, implying that he is imperfect.

You would be wise to avoid this jerk as much as possible. He is exploitative by nature and will take advantage of you in any way he can. He will expect you to shower him in praise and to reinforce his larger than life self-image. This jerk may react with rage when he is treated the same as others whom he deems inferior. He will expect special accommodations, such as not having to wait in line or being served first. And he believes his time is more valuable than yours or anyone else's.

He will probably ignore your birthday because if it isn't about him then it just isn't important enough to think about it. Unless it has a direct effect on his self-image, he is not concerned about hurting your feelings because he never stops thinking about himself long enough to consider that you have any feelings anyway. Everything about this jerk says you are

David Dasnod

not important but he is.

MALEVOLENT CRITICIZER

This jerk is always complaining about something or criticizing everything you do. His drink is too weak, or it's too strong. You don't talk enough or you talk too much. You are too heavy or too skinny. You're too intelligent or too stupid. Nothing is ever right because there is always something wrong with it.

This jerk is unhealthy to be around for very long. The criticizer habitually talks negatively about the world he lives in and everyone on it. You may catch yourself wondering why you are even listening to this imbecile. He is constantly tearing away at your pleasant attitude or your positive outlook in any way possible.

Any type of relationship with him is going to be highly caustic to your soul. He will destroy your self-esteem and confidence. This jerk will always remind you, in his critical way, that you will never be good enough for anything. Your efforts will always fall short of what he expects. He may even start telling you how fortunate you are to have him in your life because no-one else would put up with someone as useless and incapable as you.

The Malevolent Criticizer is very negative and isn't ashamed to spew out his pessimistic thoughts. He's attracted to negative conversations and criticism. He loves to watch the news because it is filled with negative energy. He soaks up negative thoughts and feelings like a black hole. He is filled with it and it foams out of his mouth every time he opens it to speak. So do yourself a favor and stay clear of this jerk's event horizon.

SADIST

Most abusers are sadistic to some degree. So it goes without saying that the sadist comes in various degrees of intensity depending on his sadistic appetite as well. However, the sadist differs from the other abusers in that he abuses others for the mere pleasure of inflicting pain and discomfort and not just as a means of manipulation.

The sadist may range from the guy with a mild sadistic sense of humor to a full-fledged monster that puts him outside the classification of a jerk and into the kinkazoid assortment. We are only going to focus on the sadist within the jerk arena here. The distinction between just being a sadistic jerk and a criminal is that the sadistic jerk may simply enjoy his sadistic tendencies but the mentally deranged appears to be addicted to his perversion.

Most sadistic jerks are capable of controlling their sadistic tendencies and seldom ever cross the line where what they do becomes non-consensual. A sadistic jerk becomes a jerk when he refuses to respect the boundaries you set. If he continues to talk about a subject you just told him makes you uncomfortable then he may not respect your boundaries in other areas either.

The sadist is still an abuser and should be avoided if you are not of the masochist persuasion. He doesn't usually just come out with a full confession about his sexual practices and preferences but there are a few cues that may let you in on his orientation.

The sadist will appear aloof, private and reclusive. He isn't too quick to let you in on his private lifestyle. The sadist gets aroused by exhibiting disrespectful, cruel and demeaning behaviors towards you. He may humiliate you in front of others by treating you as a subordinate and taking disciplinary actions. He will find it amusing when you suffer. He even finds the sounds you make while in pain pleasurable. The sadistic jerk will insist on having the final word and that word must be obeyed regardless of how senseless it is. Sadistic jerks will have a fascination with gore and violence. He loves weapons and is fixated on death and torture.

Since this jerk uses sadistic means of creating sexual arousal he may find that regular sex is just not interesting enough. If he isn't careful or well in control of his mental processes he may find himself slipping into that deep dark dungeon of perversion and crime where he will grow weird, old and alone.

STALKER

This jerk believes that he is in love with you and that those feelings are mutual. He calls and keeps calling you. He may show up wherever you are at all hours of the day or night. He may even show up at your place of work uninvited. He is likely to send you flowers or gifts every day. He will fill your mailbox with emails and may even send you some interesting videos of himself.

He may call and harass your relatives, friends, their friends, and anyone else remotely connected to your life to express just how much he loves you. This jerk is completely enthralled with you.

The Stalker tends to read more than there is into your comments or gesture and blows them out of proportion. He interprets everything you do as confessions of your devotion to your so-called "relationship" with him. He makes himself a nuisance by intruding on your privacy, disrespecting your personal boundaries and ignores how he makes you feel. No amount of rejections, warnings or inhospitable acts will convince this jerk that you are not in love with him.

This jerk is socially-inept, awkward, and may suffer

from some form of psychological disorder (to say the least). He seems to be compelled by loneliness and stimulated by fantasies. He seeks an intimate loving relationship and may believe you are his long-sought-after soul mate and that you are meant to be together by the forces of destiny. Because of this, he possesses a peculiar sense of entitlement simply because you attracted his interest.

The Stalker is a mental assailant that repeatedly disrupts your life with whom you have no relationship to speak of. The minor acts that intrude on your life by themselves may be mildly abusive but when put together they have a cumulative effect on your sense of well being.

It may be worth noting that this jerk may react to any perceived rejection by you unfavorably. When this jerk finally becomes aware that his "relationship" with you is hopeless, he may become dangerously spiteful and go off in a spree of vindictive self-destruction because you had become the only excuse for his pathetic existence.

TOSSING THE JERK OVERBOARD

If you are not careful you may find yourself involved with a jerk before you discover his true character. A relationship with a jerk is more like having an arrangement than a relationship. Depending on the extent of your relationship with a jerk it can be frustrating being with him and trying to find your way out of an ever growing invasive situation.

You may find that the quality of your life is significantly reduced when he is around. In order to do what you want to do you have to conduct your activities around the times when the jerk wants you to do things for him, therefore missing out on significant times shared with friends and family. You may find your life slowly losing any meaning as you struggle to hold on to your own values while adopting his instead. The jerk will eventually suck away your sense of significance in order to nourish his own.

Life's short and we only get so many days to enjoy the happiness that we manage to create for ourselves. There's no point in filling those days with feelings of intimidation, fear, angry outbursts, paranoid control, or other sources of drama that can leave you in a total loss of your self-esteem and self-confidence.

Don't waste your life accommodating a self-centered, immature, manipulative jerk. Pulling up anchor and sailing away from the jerk in your life could be the christening of a whole new beginning. It can be as easy as deciding not to buy the jerk sitting next to you any more drinks. You simply have to decide not to be among the casualties of a 'sinking ship' because jerks do not make good lifeboats. The best thing you can do if you find yourself on a sinking ship of jerks is to put on a life jacket and let the ship go down but make a mental note to yourself to choose the next cruise ship with a little more care.

When you decide to toss your jerk overboard (usually shortly after reading this book) you may first want to create an exit plan. This plan should consist of a series of actions you may want to take to protect yourself before sending him plunging into the cold dark waters below. Planning out your mutiny provides you time to detach any emotional strings you may have from the jerk and allows you to think over the consequences and/or benefits of your actions. Making a plan can be empowering to you. It can give you permission to imagine what your life could be like without a jerk hanging around. It may bring you hope when there isn't any.

If the jerk happens to notice you in your life raft paddling away, say you are depressed or upset about something or any other emotional condition that involves an empathetic discussion, thereby encouraging him to avoid the issue altogether.

Just remember, if you feel the need to explain your escape to the jerk expect some resistance. He will only be wondering who is going to be around to make his life easy if you leave him. If you leave, he will have to go out and find another accommodator and he won't want to do that if he doesn't have to.

Besides, the jerk will not understand how his actions are making you want to leave him in the first place. He is going to get upset if you try to explain how he is acting like a jerk and how his jerkish behaviors make you feel, so be careful. Losing his accommodator will likely make the jerk angry; anything can happen so prepare for the worse.

And don't forget, the jerk isn't concerned with how you feel or how hard this is for you. His only concern is going to be with how all of this is going to affect him. You are going to be blamed for rocking the boat. The jerk will find this sudden change to his life irritating. He is going to be confused and won't understand why you no longer want to be his little galley slave.

His fear of being cast to sea alone will transform

into despair and then into anger. But whatever form his reaction should take, it's only an attempt to manipulate you into staying with him; at least long enough for him to find a replacement. Being upset is an easy way for him to manipulate you into giving him your attention. Once he has your attention, he can start manipulating you into giving him what he wants. That is if you choose to accommodate him.

The best thing you can do once the jerk is overboard is to start making new friends, read a few good books, join some groups, start a new life and get busy doing things you like to do for a change. Learn what you can about jerks along the way and soon you will find that you no longer have any time to spend accommodating jerks.